GoNoodle®

DANCE PARTY!

The Ultimate
Dance-Your-Heart-Out
Activity Book

All rights reserved. Published by Scholastic Inc., *Publishers since 1920*.
SCHOLASTIC and associated logos are trademarks and/or registered trademarks of Scholastic Inc.

The publisher does not have any control over and does not assume any responsibility
for author or third-party websites or their content.

ISBN 978-1-338-81390-6

10 9 8 7 6 5 4 3 2 1   22 23 24 25 26

Printed in the U.S.A.   40
First printing 2022

Book design by Two Red Shoes Design
Stock photos © Shutterstock.com.

Scholastic Inc.

WELCOME TO THE

Hi there! We're the GoNoodle Champs! If you want to have a ton of fun, you've come to the right place.

Get ready to sing, dance, and GoNoodle! You'll pop bubbles, make yummy snacks, play games, and learn your favorite GoNoodle dance moves. You're going to stretch, move, think, and feel. And did we mention dance?

CHAMPIVERSE!

The activities in this book are super simple and super awesome. Some of the games, crafts, and recipes use common household items. Make sure you ask an adult for permission before doing any of these activities. That way, you'll have the safest, most fun experience. Yay!

Whether you love to party or chill out, play sports or make art, we've got you covered. All you need to do is turn the page and start the adventure.

Let's go!

MEET THE CREW

We're so excited to meet you! Tell us a little bit about yourself, too.

MC WIGGLEWOMP

I'm a breakdancing ball of energy. Bust a move!

PENNY G

I play music and make music. Let's jam!

OM PETALHEAD

I'm cool, calm, and collected. Breathe with me.

TINY O FLEXEM

You might find me odd, but I'm having fun!

NOVA STEAMSTEEN

I love science, tech, engineering, art, and math!

CHRIS SHABOB

Meet me in the kitchen! I'm a master chef.

FLO YO

I love taking shellfies on my shell phone!

SQUEAKY LAROO

I prefer to stay out of the spotlight.

RAD CHAD

Extreme sports and footie pajamas are my jam!

GULPS WODDA

I'm all about hydration. Got water?

VINCE PYLON

I'm a big fan of my fans!

TANGY BODANGY

Life is wicked awesome. Hang ten!

Name _____

Age _____

Favorite color _____

Favorite food _____

I love to _____

and _____

I'm a great _____

SQUATCHY

There's nothing I love more than rock 'n' roll!

JUST GARY

I'm a bookworm with a real passion for books.

FLAPPY TUCKLER

You know me: just busy daydreaming about unicorns!

ZAPP VON DOUBLER

I'm a genius who loves to invent things!

THE BEST TEES

We're all about positivity, kindness, and sweet dance moves!

MOOSE TUBE

Come chant and cheer along with us. Let's go!

ENMOCIÓN

We're energetic and fun, and we're here to move. ¡Vamos!

FIND YOUR CALM

Rainbow Breathing

Are you ready to fill your day with joy and movement? Let's warm up first by breathing a rainbow.

1 Sit up tall. Let your arms hang down by your sides. Open and close your hands a few times.

2 Turn the palms of your hands so that they're facing forward. Stretch your fingers out long.

3 Keeping your arms straight, slowly float them up from your sides. Feel how wide your hands can reach to the side and then up.

4 Let your arms come down and return to your sides.

5 Turn your palms out and reach wiiiiide for a bigger rainbow. Inhale and fill your lungs with air the whole way up.

6 Once your arms are up, go ahead and exhale. Relax up there. Enjoy the rainbow!

7 Make another rainbow as you bring your arms down. With your arms up, breathe in to get ready. Then breathe out and see the rainbow form as your arms float down to your sides.

8 Stand up for your next rainbow breath. Raise your arms slowly as you breathe in, reaching wide and tall. Then let your arms come down with a slow exhale. If you're feeling good, try it one more time!

Whoa, that was one nice rainbow! Now see how it feels when you match your breathing with your movement.

HOW TO!

Stretch & Strengthen

We're going to wake up our bodies from top to bottom and front to back! Grab a timer and get your moves on.

HEAD AND SHOULDERS
Neck Rolls (30 seconds)

1 Tip your head to the left, then gently roll your head back. Keep rolling to the right.

2 Roll your head forward so your chin touches your chest. Then roll your head back up to the left.

3 Reverse it! Roll your head forward to the right and back to the left.

Can you feel the stretch in your back?

ARMS
Arm Crosses (30 seconds)

1 Start with your arms hanging down by your sides.

2 Swing your right arm across your body. Then swing your left arm across your body.

3 Keep sweeping your arms through the air—from left to right, and from right to left.

LEGS
Lunges (30 seconds)

1 Step one foot forward and bend both your knees. Your back knee should be just above the floor.

2 Stand back up and repeat with your other leg forward.

3 Keep lunging and keep breathing!

That was a great warm-up!

HOW TO! Salute the Sun

Namaste! It's time to breathe and stretch! Grab a yoga mat or towel, and let's salute the sun.

STEP 1

Stand straight and press your hands together in front of you.

STEP 2

Inhale as you sweep your arms above your head, arching your back as you stretch out. Then exhale as you bend forward. Can you touch your toes?

Inhale and exhale as you step your left foot back into a lunge. Make sure your right knee is over your right ankle.

Inhale and exhale as you stretch your left foot back into a plank.

Bring your knees down to the mat. Then bring your chest down, so you're lying with your palms flat on the ground and elbows bent.

Keep your palms on the ground as you straighten your arms into a downward dog position.

Inhale and exhale as you bring your right knee forward into a lunge. Bring your left knee forward to meet your right. Go back into a forward bend, like in step 2.

Slowly inhale as you stand up. Reach your arms above your head as you arch your back. Then exhale as you bring your arms down and your hands together in front of you, just like you started.

LET'S MOVE!

The Jellyfish Song

You don't have to be under the sea to bop and blob like a jolly, jiggly jellyfish. You can do this dance anywhere!

1 Stand with your feet apart and raise your arms.

2 Bring your wrists together above your head. Keep your hands apart.

3 Keep your wrists together as you bring your arms down in front of you. Now bring your elbows together.

4 Jump to bring your feet together. Bend down with your knees touching.

Moose Tube

5 Jump again and land with your feet apart.

6 Stick your bum out and give it a wiggle!

7 Sway and stomp side to side. You're doing the jellyfish!

Dance Challenge

Can you add these moves while you do the jellyfish?

- Stick out your tongue
- Jump up and down
- Tilt your head

LET'S MOVE!

TriAngle Dance

We're going to do the triangle dance. You'll need two friends and a bunch of energy!

1 Stand in a triangle formation with your friends. Place your hands on one another's shoulders.

2 Jump in the middle of the triangle while your friends jump to either side of you.

3 Everyone jumps back to the original triangle position.

4 Then the second person in the triangle jumps in the middle while you and the other friend jump on either side.

TRIANGLE DANCE

5 Jump back to the original triangle position. Finally, the third person in the triangle jumps in the middle while the other two jump on either side.

6 Time to freestyle! Do your own thing before you do the triangle dance again.

Dance Challenge

Can you make your own moves based on these shapes?

- Square
- Star
- Circle
- Heart

7 Start over and repeat this sequence five times.

MAKE IT!

DIY Choreography

Make your own silly dance! Fill in the blanks on the next page. Use these words if you need ideas!

Word Bank

Thing	Dance Step	Description
chicken	wiggle your hips	bright
snake	clap your hands	funny
mouse	jump up and down	sparkly
cat	stomp your feet	colorful
bunny	shake your legs	kooky
dog	wave your arms	happy
bee	run in place	silly

Dance Party!

You're invited to my dance party! Everyone is going to wear a(n) _____ costume. You will dress
description

like a(n) _____.
thing

When you arrive, head straight to the dance floor! We'll do a new dance. It's called the _____.
your name

Here's how to do it. Just play _____
your favorite song

and dance along.

1. Put your hands on your _____.
part of the body

2. Then _____.
dance step

3. Next, _____.
dance step

4. Repeat these steps _____ times.
number

5. Now _____ very slowly.
dance step

6. Speed it up! _____ as fast as
dance step

you can.

Keep doing this _____ dance
description

until the song is over. Next time, can you do all these steps

in the style of a(n) _____
description

_____?
thing

LET'S MOVE!

Snack Attack

Hungry for more dancing? Work up an appetite with these tasty moves! Sing and dance along.

STOMP!

1 Stomp your foot.

SNAP!

2 Snap your fingers.

STOMP!

3 Stomp your foot.

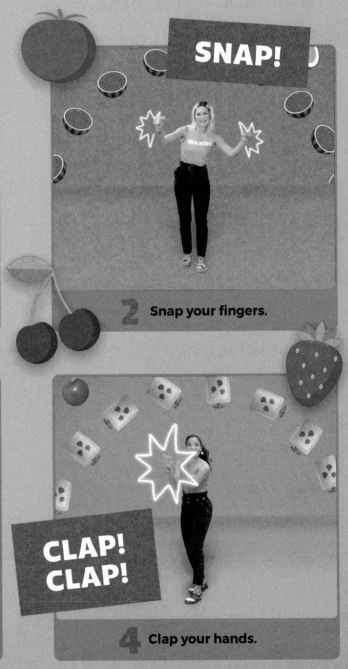

CLAP! CLAP!

4 Clap your hands.

STOMP! SNAP! STOMP! CLAP! CLAP!

5 Repeat the first three steps, then clap twice!

What time is it?
IT'S TIME FOR A SNACK!

6 Bounce and circle your arms.

What do you want?
WE WANT THOSE SNACKS!

7 Jump up and pump your hands.

What do you love?
WE LOVE THOSE SNACKS!

8 Jump and wave your arms.

Holla back,
IT'S A SNACK ATTACK!

9 Kick your left foot forward and back, then step forward!

MAKE IT!

Snack Break

Your body needs fuel to function! Get the energy you need to keep dancing and moving with a tasty treat.

- Carrot sticks—dip in hummus!
- Apple slices—sprinkle with cinnamon!
- Hard-boiled egg—peel the shell, take a bite.
- Popcorn—air-pop some kernels and add grated cheese!
- Trail mix—nuts, chocolate chips, and dried fruit. Yum!

Try this recipe for my favorite healthy snack—ants on a log!

Ants on a Log

What You Need
Celery sticks*
Nut or sunflower seed butter
Raisins

What You Do
1. Use a spoon to spread nut butter on the celery.
2. Press some raisins into the nut butter.
3. Enjoy!

You can use a banana instead of celery, or blueberries instead of raisins. Go ahead, get creative!

*Ask an adult to help you cut the celery.

20

GAME TiME!

Partner Sit 'n' Stand

In this exercise, you're going to pair up, sit down, then stand up. Grab a friend and let the fun begin!

1 Stand back-to-back and lock arms.

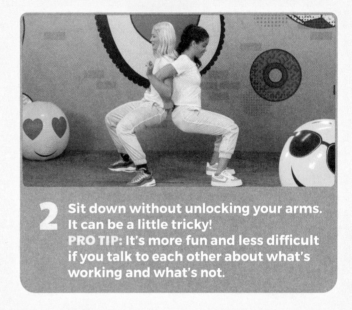

2 Sit down without unlocking your arms. It can be a little tricky!
PRO TIP: It's more fun and less difficult if you talk to each other about what's working and what's not.

3 Stand up without unlocking your arms. This part is even trickier! Keep talking and working with each other. Give it your best shot.

HOW DID IT GO?
If you were able to do it, that's great. If not, no worries! You gave it your best shot. Talk with your partner about what worked and what didn't, and try again!

LEVEL UP!
- Try to play this game with three people.
- Use a timer to see how long it takes to sit down and stand up. Can you beat your time?

LET'S MOVE!

Purple Stew

Have you ever made purple stew? No? You're about to! Sing and dance along.

We're making a purple stew.

1 Bend your legs and place your fists one on top of the other. Now move your hips and arms in a circular motion to stir the pot!

Whip whip whip whip!

2 Shake your hips and arms from side to side. Whip up that stew!

We're making a purple stew.

3 Stir the pot again, around and around.

Shoo-bee-doo-bee-do!

4 Wave your arms up and down while wiggling your fingers.

With purple potatoes and purple tomatoes.

And we want you!

5 Stick out your right arm. Then stick out your left arm.

6 Point to a friend. They can add something to your stew!

That sounds delicious!

What are you going to add to the purple stew? It could be anything—purple meatballs, purple sparkles, or purple bananas. Throw it into the pot, then keep on dancing!

MAKE IT!

Bubble Break

> Step into my lab and let's mix up some bubble formula! Ask an adult to help as your lab assistant.

What You Need
1 cup dishwashing liquid (Joy or Dawn works best)
½ cup corn syrup
3 cups water
Pipe cleaner

What You Do

1. **Whip up your bubble mix!**
   Mix the dishwashing liquid, corn syrup, and water in a bowl.

2. **Make your own bubble wand!**
   Bend the pipe cleaner into a loop at one end. The bigger the loop, the bigger the bubbles!

3. **Let's blow!**
   Dip the wand into your mixture and blow those bubbles!

Bubble Challenge

The fun isn't over yet! Here are some ways you can step up your bubble game.

- **GET CREATIVE!** String beads onto the handle of your wand for decoration.

- **MAKE SHAPES!** Twist the loop at the end of your bubble wand into different shapes. You can make a heart, a star, a square, or any shape you like.

- **BUBBLE DANCE!** Blow a bubble and start dancing! Keep moving until the bubble pops.

- **TWEAK THE FORMULA!** What happens if you make bubble mix without corn syrup? Try it and see! What differences do you notice?

- **SWITCH IT UP!** You can use a straw or an empty toilet paper roll to blow bubbles. Just dip one end into your mixture until it is completely coated. Then blow from the other end to create bubbles.

Poppin' Bubbles

Now that you've made your own bubble mix, it's time to sing, dance, and pop those bubbles with Flo Yo!

Poppin' left! These bubbles ain't so tough.

1 Start stepping to the left! Put your arms out and pull them back in with each step.

Poppin' right! I simply can't get enough.

2 Step to the right! Put your arms out and pull them back in with each step.

I'm poppin' bubbles! Poppin' high and low.

3 Run in place while pumping your arms into the air. Pump your arms high, then pump them low!

Anything is possible when you're poppin' with Flo Yo!

4 Jump around in a circle with your arms raised up.

Poppin' bubbles, pop pop poppin' bubbles.

5 Stick one leg out to the side. Point your opposite arm up in the air. Then bring your arm down across your body and point it toward your leg. Keep pointing your arm up and down. Turn on some music and dance in time to the beat!

Poppin' bubbles, poppin' on the double.

6 Reverse it! Point your other arm in the air. Bring it up and down across your body.

I got to get these fishes out of trouble.

7 Run in place while pumping your arms above your head.

So I keep on poppin'. Poppin' all these bubbles!

8 Bounce and bop side to side while waving your arms in the air.

FIND YOUR CALM

Bubble Breath

Did you know that blowing bubbles can calm you down? Try this when you feel upset, stressed, or anxious.

1 Inhale deeply through your nose.

2 Exhale slooooowly out through your mouth.

3 Keep bubble breathing. Inhale and exhale eight more times. How do you feel now?

You can use your own bubble wand and bubble mix, or you can pretend! Just breathe out slowly like you're blowing through a bubble wand. Imagine a big bubble slowly forming and gently floating away.

Another way to find your calm is by coloring! Use pencils, crayons, or markers to color the bubbles. Choose any colors you like. Take your time as you fill each bubble.

When you're finished, look at your **RAINBOW** of bubbles! Notice how you feel.

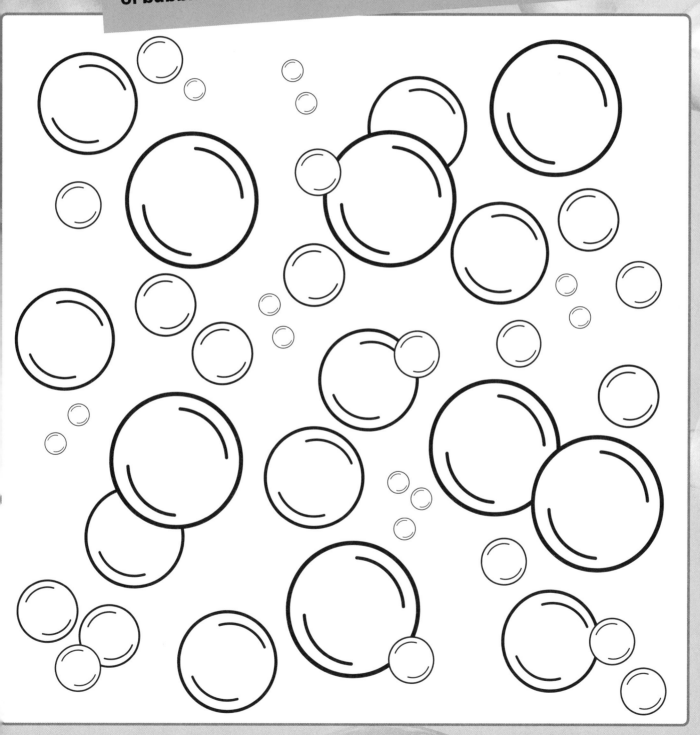

Would You Rather?

Get ready to boogie down and bust a move. When you play this game, everybody wins!

Don't stop moving!

What You Need
Paper
Hat, cup, or bowl
Pencils
A friend!

What You Do
1. Write each dance move from the list on its own slip of paper. Feel free to add your own moves!
2. Pop the slips of paper into your favorite hat or a cup or bowl from the kitchen.
3. Take turns picking two pieces of paper at a time.
4. Decide which move you'd rather do. Then start dancing!

Suggestions

clap	wiggle	disco	point
duck	jump	hip shake	bunny hop
shimmy	finger snap	spin	run in place
stomp	twirl	leap	slide

MAKE IT!

Make Your Own Microphone

If you want to rock the mic or drop the mic, it helps to have a mic! Make your very own microphone with recycled materials.

What You Need
Aluminum foil
Toilet paper tube
Colored markers, paint, or crayons

What You Do
1. Scrunch up the aluminum foil into a ball.
2. Stuff the ball into one end of the toilet paper tube.
3. Decorate the tube with colored markers, paint, or crayons.
4. Sing into your microphone like a rock star, a country rock star, a pop star, a K-pop star, or any other kind of star!

Get Creative!
- Decorate your mic with other craft supplies. You can use paint, glitter, stickers, or tape. Or glue on scraps of colored paper for a collage look!
- Make different microphones for different styles of music!
- Can you do the dances in this book with your microphone? Try it!

LET'S MOVE!

Freeze!

Here's a *cool* way to *warm* up your body in winter. Follow the steps and dance away. Whenever it says FREEZE, strike one of the poses you see and hold it!

1 Let's get started. Move your feet and sway. Then . . .

FREEZE!

2 Jump to the right. Then . . .

FREEZE!

3 Dance like a robot. Then . . .

FREEZE!

4 Slide to the right. Then . . .

FREEZE!

5 Spin around, put your hands in the air, and sing out loud. Then . . .

FREEZE!

ENMOCIÓN

6 Turn around and dance in slow motion. Then . . .

FREEZE!

Strike a pose!

Dance Challenge

Can you make your own dance for each of the other seasons?

Spring: Stretch and grow like a flower!

Summer: Splash in the waves at the beach!

Fall: Dance like a leaf slowly drifting to the ground!

GAME TIME!

Emoji Dance

Play this game to express different emotions through dance! You can do this on your own, or play with friends by taking turns. All you need is a sharpened pencil and a paper clip!

Let's go for a spin!

1. Place the paper clip on the red dot in the center of the wheel.

2. Lightly press the nib of your pencil on the red dot. Hold the top end of the pencil to keep it upright.

3. Using your other hand, spin the paper clip around the pencil nib.

4. Look at the emoji the paper clip lands on. What emotion is shown?

5. Dance in a way that expresses that emotion!

Dance Challenge

Have you ever felt different emotions at the same time? Try mashing up two emojis into one silly expressive dance!

LET'S MOVE!

Guacamole

Sing, dance, and celebrate this awesome food as you go through the months of the year. Check it out!

Guacamole! We eat it every day. Guacamole! In every single way.

Guacamole! You cannot take it from me.

1 Lean back to the left and roll your arms. Then lean back to the right as you keep rolling your arms.

2 Stand with your feet apart and waggle your finger as if to say "no!"

Three hundred sixty-five days a year. Guacamole!

3 Run in place. Then jump and land with your legs wide apart. Bounce as you wave your arms in the air!

Thirty days in September,
April, June, and November.
All the rest have thirty-one,
but February has twenty-eight.
We're done!

SEPTEMBER

30   30

4 Step one leg behind you and out to the side. Put that leg back in front, then step your other leg behind you on the other side. Keep going back and forth and from side to side!

But every leap year,
I shed a happy little tear.
An extra day of guac
is in the hemisphere.

Because February has
a twenty-ninth day.
It's a guacamole holiday!

LEAP YEAR

5 Bend your knees and bob side to side. Run both index fingers down your cheeks like they're tears of joy!

FEB 29   FEB 29

6 Rock out! Play air guitar, jump up and down, pump your fist in the air, and shake your head back and forth!

Dance Through the Year!

Now that you've danced your way through the days in each month, try this game.

> You can play with as many people as you like. It's perfect for a big dance party!

1 What day of the month is your birthday? Find it on the calendar.

2 When everybody has found their day, start playing a song.

3 Dance in the style listed on your day. Just try your best and make it up as you go!

4 Keep dancing in this style until the song ends.

Dance Challenge

How many days are in the month you were born? (If you need a hint, look at the lyrics to the guacamole song on pages 36 and 37.) Find that number on the calendar and dance in that style!

Sunday	Monday	Tuesday	Wednesday	Thursday	Friday	Saturday
1 Dance slowly	**2** Ballet	**3** Dance like a robot	**4** Tap dance	**5** Play an air-guitar solo	**6** Hip-hop dance	**7** Dance without moving your arms
8 Belly dance	**9** Totally freestyle!	**10** Dance like you're underwater	**11** Jazz dance	**12** Ballroom dance	**13** Dance like you're surfing	**14** Dance like a bird
15 Dance without moving your legs	**16** Pretend to play the drums	**17** Dance like you're swimming	**18** Hip-hop dance	**19** Wiggle like a bowl of noodles	**20** Dance like you're splashing in a puddle	**21** Dance like a dinosaur
22 Ballroom dance	**23** Hip-hop dance	**24** Jazz dance	**25** Totally freestyle!	**26** Dance without moving your arms	**27** Dance slowly	**28** Dance like a robot
29 Tap dance	**30** Dance like you're underwater	**31** Play an air-guitar solo				

MAKE IT!

Make Your Own Guacamole

It's time to rock some guac! Make some moves in the kitchen and mix up this yummy snack.

What You Need
For the guacamole:
2 ripe avocados
¼ teaspoon salt

For dipping:
Baby carrots, cucumber slices, or whole-wheat corn chips

What You Do
1. Have an adult slice the avocados in half and remove the seeds.
2. Scoop out the insides of the avocados and put them in a bowl.
3. Add salt, then mash the mixture with a fork or spoon.
4. Dip your carrots, cucumber, or chips into the guac. Enjoy!

Take your guacamole to the next level by adding a splash of lime juice, fresh cilantro, chopped tomatoes, or red onions, or all the above!

LET'S MOVE!

Balloon Party

Balloons are the best! They float, bob, bounce, shine, and POP! Here are some ways to work balloons into your next dance break.

Blow up a balloon and throw it high into the air. Dance until the balloon hits the ground!

How many different dance moves can you do before the balloon hits the ground?

Record Breaker! I did _____ dance moves. (Write the number in pencil. Records are made to be broken!)

Now try to keep the balloon afloat as long as possible by tapping it up into the air.

Count how many times you tap the balloon before it touches the floor.

Record Breaker! I kept the balloon in the air for _____ taps.

FIND YOUR CALM

Shake It Out

Sometimes if you're feeling upset or overwhelmed, it helps to shake things off. When you move different parts of your body, it can release tension and put you at ease. Get shakin'!

1 Stand up tall with your feet hip-width apart. Relax your arms by your sides.

2 Breathe in through your nose. Slowly breathe out through your nose.

3 Lift one leg off the ground and gently shake it.

4 Place your foot back on the ground. Now lift your other leg and gently shake it.

Did you know the length of your arms stretched out is about equal to your height?

5 Lift one arm out in front of you and gently shake it.

6 Lower your arm back to rest at your side. Now lift your other arm and gently shake it.

7 Stand still and slowly breathe in and out.

8 Continue to inhale and exhale for five more breaths. Notice how you feel.

This is a great way to release energy at the end of the day. Try it before you go to bed!

GO FURTHER!

What else can you shake? Build up your routine by trying these moves.

- Shake your shoulders
- Shake your head
- Shake your hips
- Shake your bum
- Shake your hands

Find Your Calm

Winding Down

It's time to unwind. Let go of all that extra energy you built up from moving, shaking, and dancing.

1 Stand tall with a little space around you.

2 Ball up your hands into fists. Maybe cross some fingers and then make fists.

3 Spread your fingers with your palms down. Circle your thumbs, around and around.

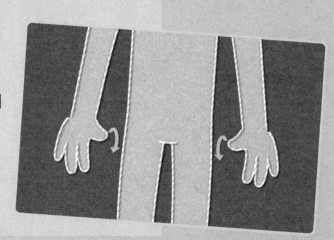

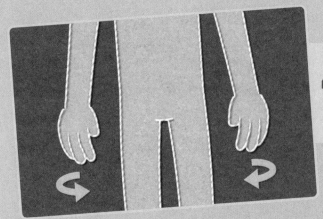

4 Circle your fingers, and just your fingers. Keep your thumbs still.

5 Circle your wrists. Then reverse the direction and circle them the other way.

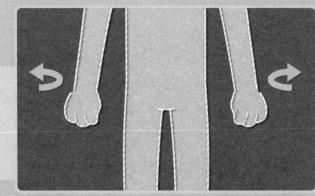

6 Next, put your elbows and your arms up with palms facing forward. Keep your elbows at shoulder height. Your forearms and hands will circle like the hands on a clock.

7 Start at twelve o'clock, then move your arms to the side to three o'clock. Go around and down to six o'clock, then up to nine o'clock. Finish where you started at twelve o'clock. Circle the clock again. Then reverse the direction. Feel yourself unwind.

8 Reach your arms high and inhale. When you're ready, slowly breathe out as you float your arms down.

How does your body feel? How do you feel on the inside? Enjoy feeling unwound!

Goodbye!

You did it! You danced and sang all the way through this book. Do you know what that means? You're a champ, too!

Take a moment to reflect on everything you've done. You got up and moved. You got creative. You're smart, strong, silly, and AMAZING.

Don't stop now! Keep filling your days with movement. Show your friends the new dances you learned. Try breathing and stretching with them. Have fun and continue to be your best self.

Bye!

YOU'RE A CHAMP!

Congratulations to

_____

(add your name here)

for dancing and having fun with the GoNoodle crew.